LAMAR JACKSON

SUPERSTAR QUARTERBACK

BY TED COLEMAN

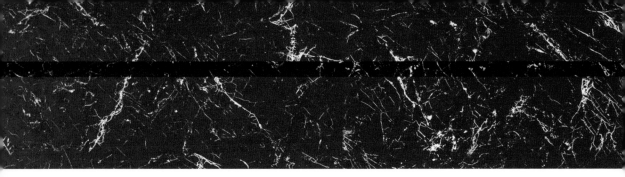

Book design by Jake Nordby
Cover design by Jake Slavik

Photographs ©: Damien Strohmeyer/AP Images, cover, 1, 30; Margaret Bowles/AP Images, 4; Nick Wass/AP Images, 7, 17, 25; Curtis Compton/Atlanta Journal-Constitution/AP Images, 8–9; Frank Mattia/Icon Sportswire/AP Images, 11; Julie Jacobson/AP Images, 13; David J. Phillip/AP Images, 14; Perry Knotts/AP Images, 19; Wilfredo Lee/AP Images, 20; Ryan Kang/AP Images, 23; Frank Victores/AP Images, 26; Shutterstock Images, 27; Red Line Editorial, 29

Press Box Books, an imprint of Press Room Editions.

Library of Congress Control Number: 2020901611

ISBN
978-1-63494-211-9 (library bound)
978-1-63494-229-4 (paperback)
978-1-63494-247-8 (epub)
978-1-63494-265-2 (hosted ebook)

Distributed by North Star Editions, Inc.
2297 Waters Drive
Mendota Heights, MN 55120
www.northstareditions.com

Printed in the United States of America
082020

About the Author
Ted Coleman is a sportswriter who lives in Louisville, Kentucky.

TABLE OF CONTENTS

1 RUNNING MAN

It was a five-yard run like Lamar Jackson had made many times before in the 2019 season. The Baltimore Ravens quarterback took the snap, extended the ball to the running back, but then pulled it back. He chose to run it himself. Jackson darted around tacklers. He weaved his way through the crowd, and he took a big hit at the end.

The run was unspectacular. But it was historic. With that simple run against the New York Jets on *Thursday Night Football,*

Lamar Jackson's running skills were on display against the Jets in 2019.

Jackson broke the record for most rushing yards in a season by a quarterback. The old record was held by Michael Vick, Jackson's favorite player growing up.

After 13 games, Jackson was just 23 yards short of Vick's record of 1,039 rushing yards. Jackson had rushed for more than 23 yards in all but one game that season, so chances were good that he'd break the record against the Jets. And he did—on the first drive.

But in the moment, Jackson wasn't thinking about the record. He was mad about the big hit he

GREAT CONNECTIONS

When he got to the National Football League (NFL), Jackson got to learn from a man who coached Michael Vick. James Urban was the quarterbacks coach in Philadelphia when Vick played for the Eagles. He later took the same job with the Ravens. When Jackson came into the league, Vick also reached out to Jackson to offer advice and stay in touch.

Jackson showed he can do much more than just run as he picked apart the Jets.

took at the end of the play. He went right back to work and stayed focused on beating the Jets. And he did it with more than just his legs.

Jackson went on to throw five touchdown passes in the game. It was the third time he'd done that in 2019. Ravens fans had come to expect great things from Jackson, no matter how he got it done.

2 POMPANO PRODIGY

Lamar Jackson was born on January 7, 1997. He grew up in Pompano Beach, Florida. Lamar loved football from an early age. When he was eight, he could already throw laser-beam passes 20 yards. By the time he was in high school, he was known for his ability to throw the deep ball.

Lamar had talent, but he also worked hard. He studied game film every week. His high school quarterback coach used to run him through four hours of drills on Sundays. That helped Lamar develop his

Lamar rushes for a touchdown against Auburn in his first college game.

arm strength. He was also super fast on his feet. Besides playing football, Lamar ran track in high school.

Lamar was a true dual-threat quarterback. He threw for 1,740 yards and 25 touchdowns as a high school junior. He also ran for 1,401 yards and 16 touchdowns. That caught the attention of many college coaches. But a lot of them saw him as a runner first. They weren't sure he could play quarterback.

But Lamar didn't want to switch positions. He was only interested in schools that would let him be a quarterback. The University of Louisville was one of those. Head coach Bobby Petrino promised Lamar that he would stay

Lamar and tight end Micky Crumb celebrate after connecting for a touchdown against Texas A&M.

a quarterback. Lamar accepted Louisville's scholarship offer.

The Cardinals were a team on the rise with Lamar. He earned playing time right away. He started eight games his freshman season. There was no doubt about his ability to run.

Lamar rushed for 960 yards and 11 touchdowns. He led the Cardinals to the Music City Bowl, where he rushed for 226 yards and two touchdowns against Texas A&M. He was named the game's Most Valuable Player (MVP) in Louisville's 27-21 win.

Lamar started the 2016 season by throwing six

FUTURE TEAMMATE

The area of Florida where Lamar is from produces a lot of football talent. He played youth football against wide receiver Marquise Brown. Brown later ended up as his teammate on the Baltimore Ravens. Lamar also played against Atlanta Falcons receiver Calvin Ridley and Las Vegas Raiders cornerback Trayvon Mullen.

Lamar poses with the Heisman Trophy after winning the award in 2016.

touchdown passes in the first half of the first game. He threw for 30 touchdowns on the year and ran for 21 more. He became the first Heisman Trophy winner in Louisville history. He was a Heisman finalist again the next season. Lamar showed he could do it all. He was ready for the NFL.

3 PROVING DOUBTERS WRONG

Many NFL teams use the 40-yard dash to measure a player's speed. But Lamar Jackson decided not to run the 40 before the 2018 NFL Draft. He didn't want teams thinking he was anything but a quarterback. He wanted them to watch his passing drills instead.

The Ravens passed on Jackson at first in the draft. They took tight end Hayden Hurst with their first pick at No. 25. Four other quarterbacks had already been drafted. But the Ravens liked Jackson.

Commissioner Roger Goodell welcomes Jackson to the NFL at the 2018 draft.

And as the first round was coming to a close, he was still available. They made a trade to acquire the last pick of the first round, No. 32. They used it to select Jackson.

It was a controversial move to some observers. After all, the Ravens already had a veteran quarterback in Joe Flacco. But the Ravens didn't want to move Jackson to a different position. They planned on him being their quarterback of the future.

The future turned into the present by November of his rookie season. Jackson had gotten a little playing time in relief of Flacco. He even threw his first career

AGENT MOM

Jackson decided not to hire an agent to represent him before the 2018 draft. Instead he had his mom for guidance. Jackson's mom Felicia served as his manager and advisor. Jackson and his mom have always been close. Jackson's father died in a car accident when Lamar was eight years old.

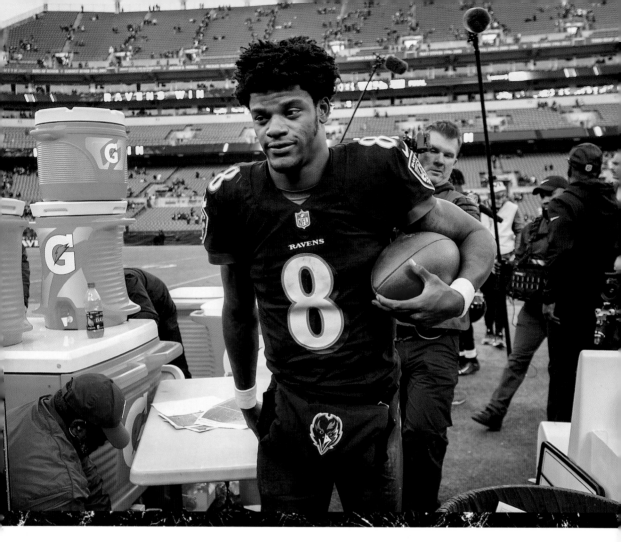

Jackson walks off the field with the game ball after his first career start.

touchdown pass in a Week 8 game. Flacco got hurt the next week. Jackson made his first career start on November 18 against the Cincinnati Bengals.

It was the first of many record-setting performances. Jackson rushed for 119 yards. That was a record for a Ravens quarterback. He also threw for 150 yards and a touchdown. Jackson turned out to be the spark Baltimore needed. He started the rest of the season and went 6–1. The Ravens finished 10–6 and won their division.

The magic Jackson had found in the regular season didn't carry over to the playoffs. The Ravens faced the Los Angeles Chargers. Jackson completed just two passes in the first half. He also fumbled twice. Some fans yelled for Flacco to come in. But then Jackson kicked it into gear. He threw two fourth-quarter touchdown passes to close the gap. But it wasn't enough, as Baltimore lost 23–17.

The Chargers kept Jackson bottled up for most of his first playoff game.

Jackson was just a rookie. He was the youngest quarterback ever to start an NFL playoff game. He couldn't wait for another chance next season.

4 HUMAN CHEAT CODE

The Ravens coaching staff saw what a special player Jackson was. They changed their entire offense for 2019 to suit him. Flacco was not a mobile quarterback. He couldn't do what Jackson did. The offense had to take advantage of Jackson's abilities.

It paid off with a historic season. Jackson posted a perfect passer rating in Week 1 as Baltimore routed Miami. He threw five touchdown passes. Jackson was doing things no quarterback had

Jackson opened the 2019 season in style with a big game at Miami.

done before. His combination of running and passing ability set records.

Despite that, the Ravens started off slowly. They were 2–2. Jackson then led them on a 12-game winning streak. Among his many achievements was another perfect passer rating in Week 10. He was just the second quarterback in NFL history to do that twice in a season. He threw 36 touchdown passes for the season. That erased any doubts about his ability to play quarterback.

Jackson was still a great runner, of course. He broke the NFL quarterback rushing record in Week 15. He finished the year with 1,206 rushing yards. He averaged 6.9 yards per carry. That led all NFL rushers, not just quarterbacks.

Jackson threw five touchdown passes in a blowout of the Rams in 2019.

The records were nice. But Jackson wanted a championship. The Ravens went 14–2 and had Super Bowl hopes. Their first playoff game was against the Tennessee Titans.

However, the Titans played giant-killer that night. Jackson just wasn't himself. He threw two interceptions. He lost a fumble. And the Titans stopped him twice on short fourth-down runs. Baltimore lost 28–12.

It was another playoff disappointment. But Ravens fans had reason for hope. They had the league's most valuable player. Jackson was a unanimous pick as the NFL MVP. He was just the second player in NFL

VIDEO GAME SPEED

Jackson was so fast that video games couldn't keep up. The Madden NFL series of games gives each player a speed rating out of 100. Jackson's was 94 before the season. But during his record-breaking year, Madden upped the ranking to 96. That made him the fastest quarterback in the game's history.

The Titans upended Jackson and the Ravens in a huge playoff upset.

history to capture every MVP vote. There was no longer any question about what kind of quarterback Jackson could be. It was just a question of whether he could make the Ravens Super Bowl champions.

SPIN ZONE

Lamar Jackson's running ability is based on more than speed. He can change directions quickly to fool opponents. His 47-yard touchdown run against the Bengals in 2019 showed off Jackson's ability to stop, cut, and avoid tacklers.

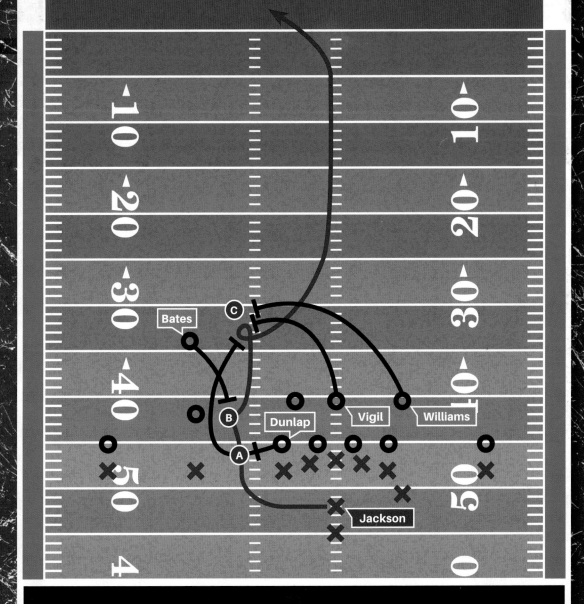

HOW IT HAPPENED

Jackson takes the snap from the Cincinnati 47-yard line, fakes a handoff, and runs upfield. He barely slips past defensive end Carlos Dunlap just beyond the line of scrimmage Ⓐ. Safety Jessie Bates closes in on him, but Jackson fakes left and cuts to his right to elude him Ⓑ.

Dunlap continues to chase Jackson, while linebacker Nick Vigil and safety Shawn Williams pursue from the weak side. Just as the three defenders close in for the tackle at the 33-yard line, Jackson plants his left foot, does a complete 360-degree spin, and leaves all three Bengals grasping at air Ⓒ. Jackson outruns the rest of the defense for a touchdown.

TIMELINE

1. ## Pompano Beach, Florida (January 7, 1997)
   Lamar Jackson is born.

2. ## Boynton Beach, Florida (2015)
   Jackson graduates from Boynton Beach High School, choosing to play college football at the University of Louisville.

3. ## Atlanta, Georgia (September 5, 2015)
   Jackson plays in his first college football game, a 31–24 loss to Auburn.

4. ## New York, New York (December 10, 2016)
   Jackson wins the first Heisman Trophy in Louisville Cardinals history.

5. ## Arlington, Texas (April 26, 2018)
   Jackson is selected with the 32nd overall pick in the NFL Draft by the Baltimore Ravens.

6. ## Baltimore, Maryland (November 18, 2018)
   Jackson makes his first NFL start, a 24–21 win over the Cincinnati Bengals.

7. ## Baltimore, Maryland (December 12, 2019)
   Jackson breaks the single-season record for most rushing yards by a quarterback.

8. ## Miami, Florida (February 1, 2020)
   Jackson accepts the NFL MVP Award, the second player ever to win unanimously.

MAP

AT-A-GLANCE

Birth date: January 7, 1997

Birthplace: Pompano Beach, Florida

Position: Quarterback

Throws: Right

Height: 6 feet 2 inches

Weight: 212 pounds

Current team: Baltimore Ravens (2018–)

Past teams: Louisville Cardinals (2015–17)

Major awards: NFL MVP (2019), Pro Bowl (2019), Heisman Trophy (2016)

Accurate through the 2019 NFL season and playoffs.

GLOSSARY

agent
A person employed by a pro athlete to handle his or her business matters.

carry
A rushing attempt.

cornerback
A defensive player who typically covers receivers.

draft
A system that allows teams to acquire new players coming into a league.

dual-threat quarterback
A player who is skilled at both passing and running.

freshman
A first-year player.

Heisman Trophy
The award given out to the best player in college football each year.

mobile
Able to move freely and easily.

scholarship
Money awarded to a student to pay for education expenses.

unanimous
Without any disagreement.

TO LEARN MORE

Books

Cavanaugh, Greg. *Lamar Jackson*. Broomall, PA: Mason Crest, 2021.

Meier, William. *Baltimore Ravens*. Minneapolis, MN: Abdo Publishing, 2020.

Whiting, Jim. *Baltimore Ravens*. Mankato, MN: Creative Education, 2019.

Websites

Baltimore Ravens
www.baltimoreravens.com

Lamar Jackson College Stats
www.sports-reference.com/cfb/players/lamar-jackson-1.html

Lamar Jackson Pro Stats
www.pro-football-reference.com/players/J/JackLa00.htm

INDEX